You Can't Make This Stuff Up: Tales From a Judicial Diva

You Can't Make This Stuff Up: Tales From a Judicial Diva

Vanessa D. Gilmore

To order additional copies of this book, contact:
Xlibris Corporation
1-888-795-4274
www.Xlibris.com
Orders@Xlibris.com
77903

CONTENTS

DEDICATION

In, 1982 my best friend, E. Lynn Harris gave me a gavel with a small note card that was inscribed as follows:

> Vanessa:
>   Went silly in Philly. Saw this and couldn't resist buying it for you. Hope you enjoy it.
>
> Love Always,
> Lynn

Lynn had supported me all through law school and celebrated with me when I accepted my first position as an attorney in 1981 by accompanying me to the law firm dinner. That is why in 1991 when he decided to leave his job as a computer salesman to pursue a writing career, I was right there for him, selling his first self-published book out of the trunk of my car at beauty shops before he was picked up by a major publisher and became a household name. And so, as I complete this book that chronicles the life that he predicted for me long before it came to pass, I dedicate this book first and foremost to him.

I also dedicate this book to my son, and Lynn's godson and namesake, Sean Harrison Gilmore, who is truly the light of my life and a fabulous source of inspiration and humor.

I also appreciate the constant encouragement of my mother Laura Gilmore and my father Clifton Gilmore and my four fabulous sister friends affectionately known as Lynn's Angels, Pamela Frazier, Robin Walters, Cindy Barnes and Lencola Sullivan.

My deepest thanks to my sister, Pamela Wilson and to my brother from another mother, Richard Montgomery, and my sister from another mister, Muriel Funches.

Finally, many thanks also go to Janet Hill Talbert for some editing help.

FOREWORD

I am a federal judge. I left a lucrative law practice to go into public service making a small percentage of what I formerly made . . . for the rest of my life. I know you're thinking why on earth would anyone do that? I remember calling my pastor in tears to tell him that I had been asked to go to the bench. He told me to ask myself two questions: 1) could I do a good job and 2) would my being a judge be good for the community? Then he told me to call him back when I had a real problem and hung up the phone.

So I took the job because I knew I would do a good job and I believed that if young girls could see somebody sitting on the bench who looked like them, that might inspire them to want to be judges. But what I didn't realize was that going from private life to public life meant that I would be voluntarily agreeing to jump into a fish bowl and put my entire life on display. Since the only thing that I had ever done that I thought might get me in trouble was tell jokes, I thought I would be easily confirmed. Then it occurred to me that my love of telling jokes and stories might actually be a problem for me. The year I was nominated to the bench, I went on a ski trip with a bunch of friends whom I entertained for an entire week by telling tasteless jokes every morning in my long underwear. I thought it was hilarious until I got home, got nominated to the federal bench and realized there was a videotape of me telling dirty jokes in my long johns. My first thought at that point was, "Oh no! Where is that videotape?" Fortunately, the tape was "taken care of" by a good friend and I went on to be confirmed to the federal bench.

I took the bench in 1994, before You tube, before reality t.v., before the internet and before the time of "judge as celebrity", so I had no earthly idea how much scrutiny I might face in this new position. I once ran across an article written about me that described me as a "judicial diva". The writer went on to suggest to readers that they try rolling my name off their tongue to see just how divalicious it sounded. With the possibility of that kind of scrutiny, you might think that I would be willing to forego telling jokes and stories, but I just can't do it.

I guess I should confess that I have an almost photographic memory when it comes to jokes. If someone names a subject, I know a joke about it. I thought that once I became a judge that life would get boring. Just the opposite has occurred, however, because during the last several years, I have encountered some of the most hilarious situations you could ever imagine. As I would relate some of these stories to friends, they would laugh uproariously and then always say the same thing. "You should write a book because nobody would believe that this stuff actually happens in real life." To which I would always reply, "Life is stranger than fiction; you can't make this stuff up." And hence the title of this book, "You Can't Make This Stuff Up: Tales From a Judicial Diva". You'll be shocked, you'll be amazed, but ultimately I think you'll be amused. I fully expect that you may shake your head in disbelief and roll on the floor laughing. But remember, you can't make up stories better than what happens in real life, so enjoy.

CHAPTER 1

It's Good to be the Judge

For many years I volunteered in the girls rites of passage program at my church. The program, formally called "Transformation", was designed to help adolescent girls transform into young ladies by exposing them to cultural, civic, educational, inspirational and religious teachings that would help them in their lives. Each mentor was assigned a girl to work with and we would take them on trips to plays and teas and sometimes to the museum. We would have classes on etiquette and history and occasionally bring in some relevant and interesting speakers as well.

One weekend we decided to do an exercise with the girls where they were each given a hypothetical profession. The information they were given was taken from a governmental web site that showed what salary they should expect to receive if they were employed in the profession they were assigned. After they got their job title and corresponding salary information, we provided them with materials they could use to develop a budget. They were given newspapers that contained real estate listings, cars for sale and grocery store specials. We provided them with ads for telephones, televisions and other appliances. We also provided them with a budget worksheet which showed them all of the various expenses they would have to budget for on a monthly basis. The purpose of the exercise, of course, was to help them relate a real world salary to some real world expenses. My mentee was given a job as a nurse and she happily sat down and started looking through the newspaper for an apartment that she could afford on her salary. I offered to help, but she wanted to work on her own.

Another young lady ran up to me excitedly and said, "Judge Gilmore, Judge Gilmore, I'm a federal judge! I can't believe how much money I make! I have so much money I don't know how I could ever spend it all!"

My first thought was, "What in the world does she mean that she has so much money she doesn't know how she's going to spend it all?"

Did the government give us a raise and not tell me about it? Is she looking at the same pay schedule that I look at every month when I am trying not to run out of money before I run out of bills?

"Let me see that," I said, taking the little slip of paper from her hand with her profession and salary designated on it. Yep, just as I thought, same crappy salary we've been getting for the last several years without a raise. This girl sure had a lot to learn about the difference between "just enough money to live" and "so much money that you can't figure out how to spend it all".

"Ok, let me help you with your budget," I said with as much enthusiasm as I could muster.

"Well, I want to pick out somewhere to live first," she said very maturely.

"Great idea," I replied.

She searched the ads for apartments and finally she announced that she had found a place that she thought she would be happy living in.

"Let me see that," I said looking at her choice of an apartment. "Oh, honey, that isn't going to do."

"But why not," she implored.

"Well, sweetie, you're a federal judge. You just can't live anywhere. That's not a nice part of town. You might end up living in a high crime area where you'll run into people you've sent to jail. In order to live in my neighborhood, you'll have to pay about four times as much as the apartment you've identified."

"What!" she screamed. "You're spending too much of my money."

"Sorry, but this is what you have to spend to live when you're a federal judge. Now what about a car?"

"Well, I thought I'd get this little Volkswagen bug."

"Oh, no honey. That won't do if you're a federal judge. I drive a Lexus. Let's see how much a car note is for a Lexus. It's probably about twice as much as you designated for your car."

"You're taking all my money Judge V. I'm not going to have any left!"

"Yes you will, yes, you will. Now let me see what else you put down in your budget. How did you arrive at forty dollars a month for entertainment?"

"Well, I like to bowl and that costs me about ten dollars every week, so I listed forty dollars for my entertainment budget."

"But sweetie, you're a federal judge. Federal judges don't bowl. We play golf."

"How much is that?"

"Well let's see. You have to join a club and that could run you about two hundred a month."

"That's not so bad."

"But wait, you also have to pay for each game you play. That's another seventy dollars each time you play. And you'll need golf clothes and shoes and equipment and they all have to be cute. My motto is that you always need to look good just in case you're not having a good game that day."

"That sounds like it costs a fortune."

"It does, sweetie. Now what else do we have to get to make the transformation to federal judge complete?"

"Well here's the grocery section. I was going to figure out a budget by using these ads."

"But you can't do that. I don't shop at that store. They don't carry enough organic products. The store I shop in doesn't generally have discount coupons so I can tell you that whatever budget you had for groceries, you can just double it to pay for organic food."

"Now I'm practically broke!"

"That's good. I was worried for a minute when you first said you had so much money you didn't know how you were going to spend it all. If you're broke, then you really are a federal judge. Congratulations, sweetie."

And who better to teach her what it means to be a federal judge than me. The most divalicious federal judge of all time!

CHAPTER 2

Stupid Criminals

After you have been a judge for a while, you get to the point where you really have seen just about everything. You have heard every excuse about why somebody buys, sells or uses drugs and you know that if you want to find Jesus, Allah or some other deity that you will have absolutely no luck if you have been looking for them in the free world because they have always "just been found" in some prison. You come to accept that it is completely reasonable for a convicted felon who is prohibited from possessing any weapon to have a handgun to protect the two-thousand dollar rims on the wheels of a car—which is sitting in front of his run-down apartment. But even after having heard it all, you are sometimes surprised to hear that there is one more thing you never saw before and never even heard about. Something that makes you put your hands on your hips and snap your neck and say, "oh no he didn't!". That moment came for me when I was monitoring a defendant's conduct after his release from prison. The federal courts have a system that allows us to release somebody from prison but still keep an eye of them as they reintegrate into the community. We do this partly to help them make the adjustment from having somebody tell them when they can use the bathroom every minute of the day to complete freedom to go when you please. We also do it to protect the people back home who understand that when they hear that cousin "Ray-Ray" is getting out of prison, it is time to lock up anything of value.

One of the things that take up a lot of our time is trying to make sure the recently released don't start immediately using drugs or alcohol. You might think that the threat of re-imprisonment would be enough to keep somebody away from alcohol and drugs, but like any addiction, it takes more than willpower to be successful. That's where we come in. We supplement willpower, or lack thereof, with constant monitoring of the ex-offenders. We try to make sure they don't accidentally go to a party where someone is smoking marijuana and unintentionally inhale second-hand smoke or that they don't inadvertently ingest some cough syrup with codeine that belonged to their cousin's son because they had a bad cold. We do this with skin, breath and saliva tests and the use of urinalysis. We understand and expect that there are times when you may have borrowed your cousins' car without realizing he had left a crack pipe in the console. When that happens we try to help you remember how important it is not to borrow a car from anyone that you suspect may be addicted to crack by putting you into a good alcohol or drug abuse treatment program where they can teach you useful things like how to recognize a crack head when you see one. But after you are given a few chances and you still don't straighten up your act, you are most likely going to have to go back go back to three hots and a cot—in other words prison.

I had one young man on supervised release who was likable enough. He had served his sentence and was trying to get his life back on track, but he had a history of drug abuse and I was monitoring him closely to make sure that he didn't become involved in drugs again. Once I order drug testing or treatment, it is the responsibility of the probation department to monitor the offenders. They do this by having them come in on a regular basis to take what we call a UA—which is shorthand for urinalysis, which we have tested by labs for any illegal drugs. Over the years, offenders have passed along all sorts of tips on how to beat the UA. One trick that is alleged to help is doing a body cleanse with cranberry juice. But the tests have become so accurate that unless you have been drug free for a while, that really isn't going to help. Some criminals would go into the restroom and water their sample down with water from the sinks or toilets which is why the toilets in those areas are now designed with shut offs for both so that there is no water in the restroom until after a sample has been given. There is even a black market out there that sells clean urine. When offenders started bringing in those samples instead of giving one of their own, a policy was instituted to require the door to be open while they are urinating to make sure we are really getting their urine and not the urine of some clean school kid with an enterprising parent. But every time you build a better mousetrap you create an opportunity for a better mouse and so it was only a matter of time before somebody came up with a way to get around the problem of no water and an open door. And thus, the "Whizzanator" was born!

I know, I know, you're asking yourself," What in the world is a whizzinator?" The short answer is a device to help you beat drug tests. The long answer is that is that it is an artificial penis that allows you to store and expel clean, reconstituted urine. Yes, you can buy dehydrated urine that you actually mix with water just like concentrated orange juice which you can then pretend to urinate out at the appropriate time to pass your drug test. It even comes with a little heater so that the sample is nice and warm just like it came from your own body. And the ladies didn't get left out on this unique and wonderful product. There is even a female version—but don't ask me how that one works. The guys who came up with this idea were making a fortune, that is until federal prosecutors got tired of them and decided to indict them for fraud. The allegation is that they are defrauding the Substance Abuse and Mental Health Services Administration by helping people to falsify information provided in federal workplace drug testing programs.

What was ingenious about this product was not just the fact that it came with a fake penis, or that it had a heater, or that it used dried urine. The most interesting selling point was that the penis was available in several skin tones including white, tan, latino, brown, and black. That is where my story starts.

As I mentioned, I had a young man whom I had sent to probation for drug monitoring. He was nice, but he certainly wasn't the brightest bulb on the tree. Somebody must have told him how he could beat the drug test using the whizzinator. Apparently though, this young man must have been in too much of a hurry to try out this new scheme. When he showed up for his drug test, he was placed in one of those special bathrooms with no water and an open door. He must have been really proud of himself that day for having thought of a way to beat his urinalysis despite the fact that he was using drugs again. Now some description of this young man is appropriate at this point and is relevant to the story as you will see in a moment. This young man was African American and I would describe his complexion as chocolatey—think Denzel Washington.

As he stood at the toilet urinating the day of his drug test, one of the officers passed by and discretely took a peek in and kept walking as is their habit. But what he saw that day made him do a double take and have to come back to the bathroom for a second look. It seems that my chocolate-colored friend was urinating with a white penis. Now how do you think this could have happened? Did he just borrow a penis from a white buddy and forget to take a look at it until it was too late and decide to take a chance? Or when he went on the web site to buy one, did he fail to notice the array of colors available for the whizzinator and just accidentally pick white? In any event, how did he think that nobody would notice that he was urinating with a white penis as brown as he was? Poor thing. Not only did he get caught, but he had to face the additional humiliation of appearing before me to explain himself. I was hoping that he might come up with some creative explanation like maybe the Michael Jackson defense. I used to be brown all over but my penis turned white due to a skin problem. In the end he wasn't able to say anything convincing. During the hearing I tried so hard not to laugh that I had to bite the inside of my jaw. Even then I ended up having to drop my head to avoid having anyone see my expression when he tried to explain why I shouldn't send him back to jail. I love my job.

CHAPTER 3

Smart Criminals

Because there are so many stupid criminals, one of the things that most people don't understand is how smart most criminal defendants are. When you look at the organization chart of a drug cartel, it rivals that of any Fortune 500 company. There are the couriers, the transporters, the logistics people, the stash house folks, manufacturers, the vehicle modifiers and so on and so on. Crime is business. Ask any correctional officer and they are sure to tell you that they have to work constantly to stay one step ahead of the inmates. The keys that the jailers carry often have key guards on them, small metal flaps that cover the teeth of the key, to keep the inmates from memorizing the tooth pattern and making duplicate keys.

Sadly though, there are many smart people who get involved in crime as a result of some type of mental illness. It reminds me of a joke my father used to tell about a guy who gets a flat tire in front of a mental institution. When all of the lug nuts from the flat tire roll away into a nearby drain, one of the residents yells through the fence and tells him to take one nut off of each of the other three tires and put them on his spare tire. He does so, but comments afterwards that he is surprised to get such good advice from a resident of a mental institution. At that point the resident replies, "I'm crazy, I'm not stupid."

I encountered a young man once whose story is reminiscent of that joke. It turns out that he was schizophrenic. He had bounced around homeless for years because of the limited number of inpatient mental health treatment options available. He had of course tried living with various friends and family members over the years, but his mental illness always made those times short lived and full of drama. After living on the streets for several years he had grown accustomed to that lifestyle. But as he got older, he realized that it just wasn't safe for him to live on the streets anymore. Then one day, he came to the conclusion he just didn't want to live at all. On that day, he decided to go to his father's house, steal a gun and kill himself. On his way there, it occurred to him that what he really wanted was to find some way to live a happy, useful life relieved of the demons that plagued him due to his schizophrenia.

He came to the conclusion that what he needed was a chance to get good mental health treatment in a clean facility where he could sleep in a bed and get three meals a day. The lightbulb went off in his head as he realized that there was a place where he could get free mental health care, a bed and food—federal prison. As he contemplated his options, he figured that robbing a federally insured bank was his best option to end up in federal prison. He abandoned his trip to get the gun and immediately went to a bank and scribbled out a note on a piece of paper—Give me the money or I will shot [sic] you. Ok, he can't spell, but other than that, his plan was brilliant. He was smart enough to know that this would get the teller's attention and likely trigger her to ring the alarm. Although he actually had no weapon, he kept his hand in his pocket pretending he had a gun. He handed the note to a teller and she proceeded to give him a bag filled with money. As soon as he had completed the robbery, he went outside and sat on the curb to wait for the police to get there. The police came immediately in response to the call, but when they pulled up, they ran right past the homeless man sitting on the curb. His look didn't fit the profile of a bank robber because he was dirty and in torn and ragged clothes, so despite his best efforts to get their attention, they completely ignored him. While the police were inside talking with the tellers, our would-be robber was desperately waiving his hands and banging on the window and holding up the bag of money for the folks inside to see. Finally, one of them noticed him and ran outside to arrest him.

As he predicted, he was indicted in federal court for robbing a federally insured institution. And with that indictment came incarceration, a bed, three meals a day, free medication and free mental health treatment for his schizophrenia. By the time I first saw him, he had been imprisoned for several weeks. He was completely lucid and mentally competent and had decided to enter a plea of guilty to the charge of bank robbery. By the time we were set for sentencing, you would have been hard pressed to detect any sign of mental illness in him. His lawyer of course argued vehemently on his behalf for a reduction of his sentence based on diminished capacity because at the time he committed the offense he was suffering from untreated mental illness. The argument is not the same as a claim of not guilty by reason of insanity, but it allows the court to take the mental illness of the person into consideration as a reason to lower the sentence. The lawyer was not arguing that he was not guilty of the crime, he simply wanted me to consider the circumstances that motivated him to commit the robbery and to take that information into consideration in determining an appropriate sentence. I was permitted to consider these arguments and was inclined to give him a lesser sentence because of the things that his lawyer had pointed out. As with every sentencing, however, the defendant is also allowed to speak in his own behalf. What I heard from the defendant that day was quite remarkable.

The defendant began by describing the history of his mental illness and how it had plagued him since he was a teenager. He talked about his parents agonizing search for an answer to his problems and the devastating discovery that he was actually schizophrenic. He described how he had spent several years bouncing from the home of one family member to another causing trouble at every stop until he finally ended up on the streets, homeless and mentally ill. Then he described how things had been for him in the weeks since he had been arrested for bank robbery. He talked about how kind the people had been to him and how thankful he was to be on medication that controlled his schizophrenia. He liked the routine of prison, being told when to get up, when to eat and when to go to bed. It seems that this sort of stability in his activities of daily living actually helped control his schizophrenia to a degree. Finally he talked about how much he hoped that I would consider his impairment in sentencing him. Oddly, however, he wanted me to give him the maximum amount of time that I could under the law so that he could continue to receive the great medical care that he had been receiving which had him feeling better than he had felt in years.

In all the years that I had been sentencing defendants, not one had asked me for more time. Everyone always pleaded with me to give them the smallest amount of time that I possibly could and this defendant was asking for the largest sentence that I could give him. I looked at his lawyer in disbelief and that is when the craziness started. His lawyer implored me to ignore his client's request and to give him as little time as I could under the law. His client responded with a vehement objection and told me that he knew exactly what he was asking for and that he wanted as much time as possible. This volley went back and forth between lawyer and client for several minutes. I felt like a spectator at a tennis match watching the ball go back and forth between two equally skilled players. More time, less time, more time, less time. Finally, I yelled "stop" so my eyes could stop bouncing back and forth and I could state the sentence. And what did I decide? Ultimately I decided to go with the defendant. The goal of imprisonment is punishment, incapacitation and rehabilitation. In the end I agreed with the defendant that those goals could be best served by a longer prison sentence. So I took one lug nut off of each of the other three tires and put them on my spare.

CHAPTER 4

My Criminal is More Stupid than Your Criminal

Judges love to talk about their cases. We like to talk about the lawyers, talk about the parties, compare notes, get advice, tell war stories and generally shoot the breeze about what we're working on at the moment. Discussions with other judges can sometimes provide you with feedback and advice that might save you a lot of wasted time and effort. Shooting the breeze with lawyers is often just another way of comparing notes. One of the things that lawyers and judges like to do is play the one-up game. My trial was longer than your trial. My jury was smarter than your jury. My legal issues were more complex than your legal issues. Occasionally, however, we are trying to one-up each other with the dumbest criminal. Have you ever seen those Darwin awards that somebody pulls together every year? People who died because they did something so stupid that you wonder how they managed to survive the evolutionary weeding out process. Well those folks don't have anything on the real life criminals we see. You haven't seen dumb until you hear us arguing about who has the dumbest criminal in cases we have actually handled.

I was having one of those sessions with a prosecutor friend of mine. I told him about a case I had involving a postal employee who kept stealing mail from the customers on her route. She had apparently become adept at identifying birthday cards and envelopes with cash in them as well as new credit and gift cards. She would pick up her mail at the station and start out on her route, but somewhere along the way, all of the good mail, that is the mail with money and gift or credit cards in them would get lost. This scheme had apparently been working for her for a while, but then some of the customers on her route started to complain about missing mail. As I related to my prosecutor friend, some bait mail was placed into her bag for delivery that contained some gift cards. She went out on her route and then apparently pulled over to the side of the road in plain view while she rifled through the mail in her truck to find the good stuff. As luck would have it, she found the planted gift cards and quickly took them for herself. She was apparently too preoccupied to notice that she was being watched the entire time and shortly afterwards she was arrested for stealing what amounted to less than one hundred dollars. Of course those small potatoes cost her a felony conviction and a very good career. I didn't think that my friend could top that story, until he started telling me his most recent dumb criminal story.

It seems that he was involved in prosecuting a bank robbery case. The prosecutor invited the defendant and his attorney to his office to see the evidence they planned to use against him in trial. In this case, as in many bank robbery cases, they had an actual video of the assailant. As you might imagine from watching cop and robber movies, most of the people who come in to rob a bank have done something to hide their faces. Often they wear baseball hats, sometimes they wear stocking masks or ski masks and occasionally they might wear a bandanna. The goal, of course, is to make it more difficult for the authorities to identify them in the surveillance video. Well in my friend's case, the robber walked into the bank in broad daylight and robbed the bank without covering his face in any way. In fact, it seems, he was almost grinning for the camera.

The defendant and his lawyer showed up at the prosecutor's office to view the surveillance video. What happened next defies all logic. As they watched the video tape, the defendant suddenly exclaimed, "Oh no. You can see my face!" The prosecutor was a bit perplexed by this statement because as I already stated, the defendant had done nothing to hide his face. Curious, he asked the defendant what he meant, trying to understand the basis for his obvious surprise. The Defendant replied that a friend had told him that if you put lemon juice all over your face that the cameras wouldn't be able to see you. He related that he had, as his friend instructed, put lemon juice all over his face, so he was totally flabbergasted to be able to see his face on the video surveillance tape.

What the hell? I guess his friend forgot to give him some of that invisible lemon juice. He must have been saving that for himself. Needless to say, my friend won the dumbest criminal contest that day.

CHAPTER 5

Flirting Criminals

Criminal defendants coming into court seek to take advantage of any opportunity they can to get a lower sentence. That is not surprising. What is surprising, however, are the lengths to which they will go to try to convince the judge to give them a lower sentence. Sometimes defendants will argue with you. Sometimes they will chastise you. Sometimes they will implore you to have mercy on them. They use their children, their sick mommas, somebody else's sick momma or anybody in the world that needs their help. Many of them bring up their good friend Jesus hoping that he will help persuade you.

I thought I had seen just about everything until one day I got surprised. A defendant came in to enter a plea of guilty on a fraud case. The first thing I noticed when he came into the courtroom was that he had to be one of the best dressed defendants I had ever seen. He had on an impeccably tailored pinstriped suit in a light color that seemed to hug every part of his very well-toned physique. He had on a freshly pressed white shirt with french cuffs and a designer tie to complete his ensemble. His shoes were highly polished, his hair was immaculately groomed and he had a fresh shave. His visual image was striking enough, but as he approached the bench he was still several feet away when the scent of his cologne overwhelmed me. The scent was so strong that my case manager who sits in a seat just below my bench actually recoiled as he approached. Now I like a good smelling man as much as the next girl, but you don't have to bathe in cologne to make a point. I was reminded of the time that one of my colleagues had to ask Jeff Skilling's lawyer to wash his face during the trial because the jury was complaining that he was asphyxiating them with his cologne.

There was even more about this guy that was interesting. As he approached the bench, he didn't just walk . . . . he kind of swaggered, almost as if he were walking down the red carpet for his close up. When he looked at me, he had this half sleepy, nonchalant look about him like movie stars who are trying to feign disinterest so you will know that they are interested. I thought to myself even before I started the proceedings, "this guy is going to be a piece of work".

The conversation during the pleas of guilty is designed to make sure that a defendant is entering a knowing and informed plea of guilty and that he is actually competent to enter that plea. We don't want anybody saying down the road, "oh I didn't know I might get twenty-five years", or I think I might be crazy so I don't think I should have pled guilty. We ask a series of questions and give them as much detail as we can about the potential outcome of a guilty plea. The first part of the discussion is mundane, what is your name, how old are you, how far did you go in school and questions like that. But from the beginning, I could see that homeboy intended to spice this thing up.

Me: "State your full name please."

Him: "Denzel Washington"

Ok, he didn't really say Denzel Washington, but the way he said his name, sort of half purring and still with that sleepy look in his eyes made me think of Denzel.

Me: "How old are you?"

Him: "I'm forty-two, your honor," he said in a kind of breathy voice.

I am wondering by now whether that is his real voice or one he has put on for me, but I keep going.

Me: "I understand you wish to enter a plea of guilty in the case now pending against you in this court."

Him: "Yesss, I dooo."

Ok, wait a minute. Hold up here. Did he kind of wink at me that time? I think he did. And not only that, he's giving me that kind of come hither look, like, "You know you want me girl". This went on for the next ten minutes. Me, playing it straight, him shaking his shoulders at me, and then speaking in a low voice, the kind that makes you have to lean in to hear him. He even licked his lips a couple of times in that sexy, let's-get-it-on kind of way. I was wondering if I was the only one who noticed. My case manager later said to me, that guy was trying to flirt with you, judge. But the question is, why?

What could possibly be the outcome of a criminal defendant flirting with me while I am taking his plea of guilty? Was he really that crazy or did he think that I might be? Did he think I might scream from the bench, "He's not guilty, Mr. prosecutor, let him go!". The chances of that happening were about as slim as the chances of Bobby Brown and Whitney Houston getting back together. Or better yet, maybe he envisioned that I would run from the bench, rip off my robe and throw myself into his arms. The chances of that happening were about as slim as the chance that Tiger Woods could convince his wife he wasn't cheating. Or probably, he thought that whenever I sentenced him I would say,

"This brother is too fine to go to jail for too long, so I'm going to give him a break." Again, not likely unless I had lost my ever loving mind. Since there was not a snow balls chance in hell of me doing anything other than taking his plea and sending him right to jail for the appropriate amount of time, I never could figure out his motivation. But I guess to him, on that day, he imagined that anything was possible. It had probably worked for him on many occasions in the past. The irony is, that when he gets to prison, that pretty boy act will actually work against him. Someone is going to rip their robe off and jump into his arms but it won't be a pretty, diva-like judge!

CHAPTER 6

Criminals Completely in Love with the Judge

If you think that Mr. Flirty was a piece of work, he doesn't begin to compare with the prisoners who actually take the time to write to me. Something about being able to hide behind pen and paper makes people, even inmates, feel less intimidated about expressing their amorous intentions. And people with a whole lot of time on their hands can really go overboard when it comes to penning their thoughts of love. Some acknowledge that they know they shouldn't write to me, but claim that their heart wouldn't let them pass up the chance. Others say that God told them they had to write me to express their thoughts of love.

For many years I had one suitor who was truly a gifted artist. For every holiday he would hand paint me a card for the occasion. My assumption is that he read some article about me somewhere that must have mentioned where I attended church because even though I have had the same, very public, work address for many years, he would send cards to me at my church. The ladies in the church office opened the first such card and then forwarded it to me with a note indicating that it had been opened before they realized it was addressed to me. But for years after that, every card he sent me that he mailed to the church was already opened when I received it. I think that the ladies were just curious after that to see if he and I were really having a little love affair. Now of course that didn't really make sense, because if we were, I would presumably have given him my real address, but in any event that is how it worked. He sent me hand painted cards for New Year's, Easter, Christmas and even a Thinking of You card. I have to say that I was impressed by his art work if not his amorous intentions. Finally he invited me to come meet him face to face for a visit. I never made the trip and he stopped sending those beautiful cards. Sometimes I wonder who the lucky woman was that became the new recipient of his artwork.

Another suitor was one of the most creative I have ever encountered. His correspondence to me was entitled "Writ of Meaningful Friendship" and it went like this . . . .

I, _____ do bring before this court a heart full of love and ask this court, based on the points and authorities filed herein that this declaration of friendship be granted . . .

Ok, you have to admit this was kind of clever, but it got better.

Now after reviewing the facts of her life and the facts of his life, plaintive (sic) can see that there are some differences, as the "sides of law". He is found to have violated the laws of California Penal Code 666, 484e and 4849. She was found to be a judge of a highter (sic) court, who sens (sic) people to prison. But all is not lost.

All is not lost? Is he on crack? Maybe he is. I decide maybe I should look up those California penal code provisions before I read any further, but I am too curious now, so I keep reading.

He tells me that he just wants to share rounds of talks because he is a good reader and a good chest (sic—or maybe he really meant he is a "chest") player. He concludes by saying the following . . .

> In the District Court of Lonlyness (sic) Rule 50-50 (L) . . . if [the declaration] should be granted for full friendship and a life long friend, who pomise (sic) to writ(sic) as often as she can. If denied, Plaintive (sic) will spin (sic) a life time of lonlyness (sic), with no corse (sic) of appeal.

I was impressed with his creativity (if not his spelling). It was the first time I almost felt compelled to at least acknowledge that I had received his correspondence. When I mentioned this to a friend of mine who was a judge in California, and told him where the guy was imprisoned, he said, "Are you crazy? That guy is in Pelican Bay. That prison is for the worst offenders in the system—for people who are on 23 hour-a-day lockdown because their crimes are so heinous. Of course he wrote you something creative. He doesn't have anything else to do. He doesn't need your thanks or acknowledgment." Okey, dokey then, I thought, never mind. Petition DENIED!

But some of the people who wrote me apparently had standards they weren't willing to compromise even though they were in jail. To be sure that I met their exacting standards, they would sometimes send me letters designed to screen me to be sure that I was the kind of person that they wanted to be involved with. I heard from one guy who sent me such a letter. Enclosed with his letter was a picture of his entire family visiting him at the prison for Christmas. It was labeled on the back to indicate the names of all of his family members. Interestingly he also took the time to identify himself, even though he was the only one in the picture with prison greens on. I probably could have guessed which one he was from the prison attire, but I suppose he figured, why take the chance.

Then to be sure that I was really the right woman for him, he sent me a questionnaire to complete. The questions included the following:

What is your religion?

Do you have a male companion (because I guess he didn't want any two timers)

Do you have a car? (the better to visit me with, my dear)

Do you drive?

Do you have a telephone? (I wondered if this was a real question)

Do you have any pictures of yourself?

Do you smoke? (I guess this was a deal breaker)

Do you like kissing in public (like in the visiting room of a prison)

These were just a few of the questions he posed from a very lengthy list. But to be fair, he anticipated that I might have a few questions of my own and answered a few questions for me as well. He revealed, for instance, that he was serving a sentence of thirty-six years, but hoped to have his sentence overturned on appeal. He described himself as a scorpio, six foot two with a slim build and wavy hair. He said he didn't want to sound conceited, but wanted me to know that he thought he was fine. And I guess if those things were my only criteria for a relationship, then my search was over. He ended by asking me to send a full length photo of myself. I decided that was an offer I could refuse.

Someday my prince will come . . . that is if he isn't already in jail!

CHAPTER 7

Trying to Make a Connection Any Way You Can

While some defendants think that flirting is the way to a judge's heart, others are not so naive. That doesn't stop them, however, from trying to make a connection with the judge any way they can. If the wink and cologne won't do it, then maybe appealing to a judge's motherly instincts will work. I can't begin to tell you the number of times that a defendant said to me that since I was a mother, they know I would understand their desire to be with their children instead of going to jail. Or that all they wanted was a chance to raise their children and teach them right from wrong the same way I was doing with my own kids. One woman even stood in front of me during her sentencing holding her newborn baby who couldn't have been more than two weeks old. And almost anybody who has kids and a willing partner will have the children sit in the courtroom during sentencing looking sadly at the judge. The problem is, these people didn't do their research on me. I didn't have any kids for the first seven years I was on the bench and I wasn't particularly moved by those sad little puppy dog eyes. I was never moved by crying babies. In fact, when my own son was a baby, I taught him sign language from a book called "Teach Your Baby to Sign," so I wouldn't have to decipher which cry meant what. I didn't put much stock in a request to be with their children when the person in front of me wasn't paying child support or even worse, was selling drugs to other people's children.

No kids, then how about your womanly instincts. This attempt for me came from a case involving a woman who had embezzled three hundred thousand dollars from a bank where she worked. It seems that she had decided to have an affair with the president of her branch. He was married and she was single. He told her that every time they had sex, she needed to give him two-thousand dollars for the pleasure of his company. Now I already know what you're thinking. This woman must have been a dog, but you would be wrong. For a while, she got cash advances on her credit card to satisfy her amorous lover. When she ran out of credit, she started stealing it from his bank. It was an expensive habit. Think about how many times two thousand goes into three hundred thousand dollars. Anyway, at some point he recognized what she must have been doing, but she stupidly stated on tape that she got her money from a personal injury settlement, so that let him off the hook. She, on the other hand, went straight to jail. I was curious about what had happened to all the money and our exchange at the hearing went something like this:

Me: "What happened to all that money?"

Her: "I gave it all to him, your honor. But, being a woman, I know you understand."

My head started spinning like Linda Blair in the Exorcist. Her thought was that I was supposed to relate to her because I should understand why an attractive, intelligent woman with a good job would pay a man two thousand dollars a pop to have sex with her?

Me: "No, I don't understand. Frankly, I've never paid for it myself. In fact, if you had worked it right, you probably could have gotten somebody to pay you for it instead."

I caught my law clerk out of the corner of my eye shaking her head in disbelief. Oops, did I just say that? Suggest that she would have been better off working as a prostitute? My bad. But frankly, she would have gotten a lot less time if she did.

One prisoner that was appearing in court on a civil rights case used a break during the trial to tell me that he had seen my picture in an Ebony magazine article. He wanted to be sure I understood how much he had liked it. Not to be outdone, another prisoner that he had brought with him to testify on his behalf chimed in that he liked my picture too. Oh joy, I thought. I'm the pin-up girl in the prison. I thanked them both for their comments, but thought it was best not to engage them in too much conversation about what they were doing with my picture in the prison.

If none of those approaches works, then pulling out the race card could be a last resort. I had to sentence one woman for her involvement in a hot check-cashing ring. Her defense at sentencing was that her husband had told her to do it and that I should understand, that as an Asian woman, she had no choice but to follow her husband's orders when given. Huh? I guess my response was supposed to be, "Well, why didn't you just say so. Of course as an Asian woman you didn't have any choice but to commit the crime your husband told you to commit. You're free to go."

Instead I gave her a piece of advice for future reference, "Just say no."

CHAPTER 8

I wrote a song about it. Wanna hear it? Here it goes.

Sometimes you run across people who have so much drama in their life that you just want to call up a reality t.v. show producer and tell them about these folks. I had one such guy whose middle name should have been drama. Somehow he had gotten "caught up" (that's slang for I really committed the crime but I don't actually want to take responsibility for it) in a counterfeit money operation. Given the non-violent nature of this offense and his background, I allowed him to remain free on bond while his case was pending. The thing about bond is that most people want it and will do anything within their power to make sure their judge doesn't revoke it and send them to jail while they are awaiting the trial of their case. This guy, however, was the exception to the rule.

From the very beginning he was just determined to rock the boat. Instead of just working hard and keeping his head down, he decided to go online and find himself a new woman. Amazing as it may seem, there are actually women out there who will begin new relationships with men who are about to go to prison. This guy wasn't entirely truthful in his personal profile, however. In fact, in reading the profile he wrote, I actually thought—hey this could be somebody I might . . . introduce a friend to. His tag line was "King Solomon seeks the Virtuous Woman". He described himself as an athletic man who didn't smoke or drink, with a good income and an interest in community service, family, religion and spirituality. He said that the most important thing is morales (sic) and values that a woman has because he was looking for an old school love like his grandparents had. He neglected to say, however, that he was on bond for a counterfeiting charge and likely to be imprisoned in the near future, but I guess he subscribed to the don't ask, don't tell policy.

Apparently nobody asked him that and soon afterwards he found a woman to spend his life with, or at least as much of his life as he had left until he was sentenced to prison. She must have figured out pretty quickly what was really going on with him, because she dumped him in fairly short order. Not satisfied to just let her go and find some other unsuspecting victim, he decided to terrorize this woman for having the nerve to reject him. First he went to her place of business and harassed her by telling her supervisors all kinds of personal things about her and then refused to leave when asked to do so. When that didn't do enough to interfere with her life, he decided to take his reign of terror to her home. One evening he called the police to report that his "girlfriend" was at home and was about to commit suicide by shooting herself with a gun. That would have been a nice gesture to try to save her, except it wasn't true.

This poor woman had just gotten comfortable in front of the t.v. with her dinner when her front door was burst open by the police. "Don't do it", they were said to have yelled at her. She was startled first, because someone had broken into her house and more importantly, because she had no idea what they were talking about. She stopped mid bite and looked at the officers with a mixture of fear and shock before she told them she had no idea what they were talking a bout. When they explained that someone had called to say that she was about to commit suicide and that they were there to save her life she knew immediately that her misfit match was behind it all. She assured the officers that she had no intention of killing herself and they left.

Apparently not satisfied with the level of commotion he had already caused her, the would-be suitor then called the fire department with the same story. Again, just as she was getting settled back to her meal, the door burst open again with fireman yelling for her to stop. This was more than this poor woman could take. She notified me of his amorous misadventures and I promptly revoked his bond.

Finally the day of sentencing came. Sentencing is a very formal process in which the judge reviews information that has been provided about the defendant and addresses any inaccuracies in that information that might have an impact on sentencing. Afterward the defendant's counsel usually says a few words on behalf of his client, emphasizing anything that might help their client to get a more favorable sentence. After that, the defendant has an opportunity to speak on his own behalf. Defendants usually use this opportunity to address the court and express remorse, say what they have done to try to improve themselves, talk about their goals for the future, offer apologies to the court, their families, the prosecutor, the Unites States and almost always to God. Basically this is the defendant's one shot to try to impress the judge before they are sentenced.

This particular defendant decided that what he needed to do to impress the court was to write a song about his misadventures, send it to the library of congress to get it copyrighted and sing it to the judge at the time of sentencing. When I asked him if he had anything he wanted to say in his own behalf, he informed me that he had written a song that he wanted to perform for me. Before I could close my mouth from utter disbelief, he starting banging on the table to get a beat going and started singing a rap song to me. It started like this . . . .

> I been to juvenile and boot-camp to (sic),
>
> Never mine (sic) my parents and stayed in trouble in school.
>
> I was in the county jail, court A elevators,
>
> Back in them days I was a young gladiator.

I looked at his lawyer who by that point was just hanging his head, completely embarrassed. When I caught his eye, he just shrugged. What was he to do at that point after all? Whatever damage there was going to be from this escapade was already done, so he might as well let the guy finish his masterpiece. Just when I thought it couldn't get any more bizarre, he began a part of the refrain that he wrote especially for me, documenting our recent history in his case.

> Venessa (sic) Gilmore is my judge on my federal case,
>
> Standing with my attorney, looking her in the face.
>
> She denied my bail and the D.A. agreed,
>
> I met a woman on the internet who lied about me.
>
> I'm revoking your bond, it might not seem right,
>
> But I can't let you hit the streets with all this drama in your life.

The song continued on for a while talking about how the secret service had discovered his little counterfeiting operation and how sad he was to have used up his allotment of phone minutes because he couldn't talk on the phone now. Finally, he got back to the chorus which he repeated periodically throughout the song . . .

> I'm changing my life
>
> Oh yes, I am!!!
>
> I'm changing my life, Lord help me Jesus Christ,
>
> I'm down on my knees, I'm begging you please,
>
> Help me change my life and help me to stay free . . .

When he finished, I didn't know whether to clap or come down off the bench and give him a high five. I sat silent for so long that he was compelled to tell me that was all he had to say. He then handed me a copy of the song for me to keep as a souvenir. I thanked him and then turned to the prosecutor who was looking at me with disbelief. The prosecutor was speechless and so it was time to sentence him. I gave a sentence that was appropriate based on his criminal activity and that was within the applicable guideline range for his crime, but judging by his reaction, I think he believed that the song was going to be enough to get him a pass. He wailed and hollered so loudly that I thought someone had died. His poor wife (yes, by now he had found someone to marry him while he was incarcerated) was in the back of the courtroom and she promptly fainted. I had to call the nurse to come see about her, but in the meantime, the defendant would not stop wailing and crying. I had him taken to the jury box, but he promptly threw himself on the floor between the chairs and the wall and refused to get up. He was so big and the position that he was in was so awkward that the marshals couldn't get him up off the floor. The marshals were yelling at him to get up, the nurse was frantically trying to revive the wife and the defendant was still screaming that his life was over. As I left the courtroom to get away from all the commotion, all I could think was that I should write a song about all this.

CHAPTER 9

The King

Pro Se is a term that refers to a person who represents himself without the benefit of counsel. There are usually only two reasons that a person would represent himself in a lawsuit in federal court. One would be that they have a legitimate case, but only a small chance of recovering enough money to make it worth a lawyer's time to represent them. The other would be . . . how can I say this gently . . . is that they are one taco shy of a combination plate. Most pro se litigants fall into the latter category unfortunately and they are often the bane of a judge's existence. They generally file voluminous nonsensical pleadings full of accusations that somebody is bugging their house or trying to destroy their lives with mind control. Most describe how they combat these forces of evil by covering their windows and doors with aluminum foil.

Many such people file civil lawsuits trying to recover money from the federal government for all the harm that has been inflicted on them. On one very rare occasion, however, I had a defendant in a criminal case tell me that he wanted to represent himself in his criminal trial. Having a defendant represent himself in a criminal case can be a nightmare. They don't know the rules of evidence or procedure, but the law still holds them to the same standard as if they actually knew what they were doing. Unlike civil cases where money is the issue, their freedom is at stake in a criminal case. If a criminal defendant insists on representing himself, however, and there is no question regarding their sanity, I give them a strong admonishment about the dangers of doing so and require them to acknowledge that they understand those risks. I also request that the defendant allow me to appoint standby counsel, that is, an attorney who will help a defendant understand the rules as the case is proceeding and be on standby to help them deal with any complex issues. Thankfully, this one defendant agreed to let me appoint standby counsel for his trial.

When the first day of court actually arrived nothing could have prepared me for what I saw when I came into my courtroom. The defendant was dressed in very elaborate purple and gold African style robe that looked like it had come from the costume department of an over-the-top movie. The gentleman also wore a hat that was shaped sort of like a crown with complete with jewels. Hanging around his neck was a very large jeweled necklace that seemed to match the jewels on his, uh, crown. I didn't want to say anything because of course if this was his ethnic attire he was certainly entitled to wear it in court, but if he had actually been represented by counsel instead of just having one on standby, there is no way in the world that his lawyer would have let him come into court dressed like that before a good ol' Texas jury.

If this wasn't already weird enough, what happened next really took the cake. I asked for each side to introduce themselves for the record. The prosecutor stated his name. Then I turned to the defendant so he could introduce himself. After making an exaggerated bow to the court, he introduced himself as King so and so. When I asked for clarification, he explained that he was actually a king of some sort and that he wanted to be addressed as such during his trial. And it is for such times as this that a judge is overjoyed to have appointed standby counsel. I immediately looked at the lawyer imploringly and getting my cue, he asked for a break and turned to speak to the "king". I could tell that the standby counsel was trying desperately to explain to the king that this was just not the right approach to take in this case. I could also tell that the king wasn't buying it. He shook his head vehemently and then finally turned back to me and said that he was ready to begin the jury selection. I explained to him the dangers of him presenting himself to the jury as a "king"

Houston is a diverse city to be sure, but the federal courts draw their jury pool from a 100-mile radius so there was sure to be at least one farmer and a couple of truck drivers from the far-flung corners of our geographic region on the jury. I didn't think that every member of the jury would appreciate his defense that "since he was a "king" he couldn't possibly have committed the crimes of which he was accused. He was unfazed by my warnings to tone it down a bit. In fact, he seemed insulted by my suggestion. So we proceeded as he requested. I called the jury and proceeded to announce the case of the United States of America vs. The King.

Of course as I expected, the jury appeared to be aghast throughout much of the trial. It wasn't just the fact that he was attired in ethnic looking clothing. Houston is, after all, an international city and people are not surprised to see others wearing clothing from different cultures. It was the fact that throughout the trial he referred to himself as the king and that he chastised anyone who would not address him as such during questioning. When the case was over, I think he was genuinely surprised when the jury found him guilty of the charges against him. The only thing that could have made that trial any weirder would have been if the rest of his court and ladies in waiting had shown up.

CHAPTER 10

The Real King

One case I had was entitled Elvis Presley Enterprises versus the Velvet Elvis. It seems that there was a dive of a bar in Houston that had made the mistake of naming itself the Velvet Elvis. The name was derived from the fact that the decor in this tacky little joint was mostly velvet paintings. Houston is one of those kind of towns where you can drive down the road and get a velvet painting of just about anything you want (because of course everyone wants a six by eight foot picture of a tiger on velvet in an ornate gold frame hanging in their living room). This establishment had a velvet Stevie Wonder, a velvet John Lennon and a velvet Ray Charles. No place would be complete, however, without a velvet Elvis Presley. This place was complete and so proud of the velvet Elvis that it decided to name the bar in his honor. That was their mistake it seems.

The folks from Elvis Presley Enterprises apparently weren't as tickled about having Elvis' name attached to the little bar as the owners were. So they sued the Velvet Elvis. Their position was that a patron might actually get confused and think that this bar really had something to do with Elvis Presley. The owners of the bar argued that the name was obviously meant as a joke and believed that nobody would mistake their little bar for anything having to do with the real Elvis. The menu did feature a caption which read "The King of Dive Bars" and offered a frozen drink called "Love Me Blenders" and food items such as peanut butter and banana sandwiches and "Your Football Hound Dog". Despite the fact that all of these references were meant to be tongue in cheek, the bar owners could not convince the Elvis Presley folks to let them have their little joke, so the case went to trial.

From the beginning the case was destined to be hilarious. The Elvis Presley folks came to court loaded for battle to protect their exclusive right to license the commercial use of Elvis Presley's name, image and likeness. Among their witnesses was a woman who was in her forties and testified that she had been to Graceland more than fifty times. I guess that meant that she went there for every vacation she had ever had which to me was quite amazing. She actually got teary eyed on the witness stand as she described her visit to the Velvet Elvis bar. Her story was that she was mortified to see velvet portraits of naked women on the same wall as pictures of the king. My first question was to seek a clarification of whom she was referring to as the king. Her response was that anytime anyone heard "the king" that they would automatically know that the reference was to Elvis Presley. I advised the witness that my first thought was of Jesus Christ, but that was just me. My second and third thoughts were of Burger King and Budweiser, the king of beers. I wanted to be sure that we were on the same page. We obviously weren't.

At some point in time one of the witnesses for the Velvet Elvis made some reference to Elvis dying on the toilet of a drug overdose, to which there was a vehement objection. The problem was that when he objected, the Elvis Presley lawyer didn't actually make a legal objection. He just objected to the witness saying that Elvis had died on the toilet of a drug overdose. I truly didn't know how to rule. If I sustained the objection did that mean I agreed that was not the way Elvis died? If I overruled the objection, was I indirectly slandering the good name and enduring image of "the king"? I felt like I was caught in the middle of some strange alternate universe where rock and roll singers were reincarnated as saints. I took the easy way out and simply asked the lawyers to move along with the testimony.

When the case was finally over, I had to make a ruling. To motivate me as I was writing my opinion, I decided to buy an Elvis Presley greatest hits cd. As I wrote, I listened to the music and then it hit me. Copyright and trademark cases are generally dull and boring, but this opinion involving "the king" should have a little excitement. I started out my opinion by stating the main legal issue, that is that liability would depend on whether Defendants improperly utilized the Elvis image or name in their business, but I described the legal problem as a need to determine whether "Defendants stepped on Plaintiff's blue suede shoes". After discussing the Plaintiff's claims against the Defendant's I noted that the Defendants had replied "Don't be cruel".

My legal analysis was that the Defendants use of the name Velvet Elvis for their bar combined with the bar's gaudy decor were a part of a parody of the faddish, eclectic bars of the sixties. I found that the phrase "velvet Elvis" had a meaning in American pop culture that was greater than the name, image, or likeness of Elvis Presley in that it symbolized tacky, cheesy velvet art, including, but not limited to velvet Elvis paintings. In other words, I found that the use of the name for the bar was, as the Plaintiffs had argued, just a joke. At the end I ordered that the opinion should be sent to the parties at their last known address and if they couldn't be found it should be "Returned to Sender". I concluded by saying "Thank you. Thank you very much."

I thought it was funny, but that's just me. The court of appeals disagreed and found that the Defendants were actually trying to convince patrons that Elvis had not left the building. The bar ultimately changed its name to the Velvet Melvin. I don't even know who Melvin is. At the end of the day, all I can say is, "Long live the king", whoever that is.

Chapter 11

Why You Shouldn't Give Your Child the Middle Name Wayne or Lee

Texas is the death penalty capital of the country having conducted 405 executions from 1976 to 2008. Harris County Texas, where the city of Houston is located, has the distinction of having the largest number of death penalty cases of any city in the country. One hundred two executions during that same time period came from Harris County. According to one analysis, if Harris County were a state, it would rank second only to Texas since there have been more executions from this one county than from any of the next nine most active death penalty states. Consequently, the federal judges of Houston receive more death penalty habeas petitions than any other group of federal judges in the United States.

A federal death penalty habeas petition is one of the last possible appeals that can be filed after a person is condemned to death. In considering a habeas appeal, if a judge believes a defendant's constitutional rights have been violated, they may send the case back to state court to have the defendant released or tried again.

At any given time, each of the federal judges in Houston might have six to seven death penalty habeas petitions pending. In fact, the Houston judges have so many death penalty cases that we have our own separate law clerks just to help us with our death penalty cases. The lists of all death penalty habeas cases pending in our court comes to us periodically and contains the names of the condemned and their dates of execution. This helps us keep track of the cases on our docket. The cases are not listed by judge, however, so you have to review the entire list to find the cases that are assigned to you. As I reviewed this list periodically over the years, I began to notice something very odd. There seemed to be a disproportionate number of petitioners on our list with the middle names of Wayne or Lee. Over the years I began to wonder to myself whether this was just some strange coincidence.

Finally, one night when I couldn't sleep, I went online to look at the website of the Texas Department of Criminal Justice to look at the names of the people that had been executed in Texas. Other people count sheep, but I decided to count the number of executions in Texas. As it turns out, Texas has executed four hundred fifty eight people since 1982, shortly after the death penalty was re-instituted. I painstakingly looked up each of those four hundred fifty eight people to determine what their middle names were. It turns out that twenty-two of them had the middle name Wayne or Dwayne and twenty-five of them had the middle name Lee. The next two most popular middle names were Eugene and Ray tied with nine each. But that meant that a full 10 percent of the people on death row had the names Lee or Wayne. I could just imagine their mammas standing on the back porch yelling for them to come in for supper . . . "Terry

Lee, get in here" or "Alvin Wayne, did you wash your hands?" all the while shaking their heads about why their children were always in trouble.

I was so intrigued when my speculation about the names turned out to be true that I decided to do an internet search on the name Wayne. Ok, by now I'm sure you're wondering why I just didn't go to sleep. But I couldn't help myself. It turns out that even though I may be the only person who has scoured the death penalty executions in Texas looking for Waynes, I am not the only one who has noticed this strange coincidence of numerous criminal defendants with the name of Wayne. It seems that there are in fact several articles on the web discussing this very fact including some that actually document the names of people with the middle name Wayne who have been convicted of violent crimes. Some of the more infamous ones include John Wayne Gacy, John Wayne Bobbitt and Elmer Wayne Henley of Houston, Texas.

As I started mulling over this information, I went back down memory lane trying to remember if there were any Lees or Waynes in my own past. I even went so far as to pull out some old year books trying to see if there might have been any early warning signs among my own classmates. Believe it or not, I found one Wayne and my first thought was that I always wondered if he would end up in trouble. Now I wonder what happened to him. Then I remembered that my best friend from high school dated a guy named Wayne who was really cute, but had already gotten in trouble by the time we were in the tenth grade. If two Waynes from one high school with a propensity for trouble is statistically significant, then I really might be on to something.

Some writers opine that the propensity for criminality among the Waynes might be connected to a 50's era affinity for macho men like John Wayne (whose given name was actually Marion Morrison). A 2006 New York Times article suggested somewhat tongue in cheek that you shouldn't let your daughter date anyone with the middle name Wayne. There wasn't much written about the middle name Lee except one interesting piece that suggested the middle name Lee made you more likely to be a victim of crime. Neither that writer or I have done any statistical analysis to back up that claim, but at the end of the day, I think it is probably wise to avoid giving your children the middle name of Lee or Wayne. And mammas, don't let your daughters grow up to date anybody with a middle name of Wayne or Lee either!

Chapter 12

Oral Argument

Patent infringement cases are interesting but challenging. They require a judge who chose to go to law school because they didn't really like math or science to analyze the technical claims in a patent written by somebody with an advanced degree in engineering and tell them what they really meant when they wrote those claims. To put it mildly, most judges hate this part of the job. But occasionally a judge is asked to review an invention that is so unique and interesting that she forgets the fact that she knows absolutely nothing about engineering, math or science and gets lost in the wonder of exactly what marvelous benefits this invention could bring to mankind.

One day I was asked to examine and analyze a new invention called the "Tongue Joy". The actual item resembled a miniature dumbbell about three quarters of an inch long with a metal rod in the middle and cylindrical pieces on both ends of the small rod. This device was the subject of a very heated lawsuit, but when I first looked at it, I had absolutely no idea what it was or what it could be used for. The attorneys picked up on my confused expression and asked to approach my bench. Without hesitation and with the utmost seriousness, the attorneys explained that the "Tongue Joy" was a miniature vibrating device that could be inserted into a pierced tongue and used for, let's just say, stimulation. Well, after I picked my jaw up off the bench I tried to listen in earnest to their presentations. To this day, I don't know how I got through it without bursting into laughter.

Before that day, I had always wondered why people pierced their tongues. Not long after I started working on this case, I was standing in line to check into the Ritz Carlton in Atlanta when I sensed that someone was standing behind me. I think it was the cologne that actually made me turn around to see this other guest who was waiting to check in. To my surprise, it turned out to be Malcolm Jamal Warner, who had formerly played Theo on the Cosby show. Since I was looking right into his face when I turned around, I felt obliged to at least say hello. So I commented that I liked the smell of his cologne. He replied, "It's Bulgari for men" in this really slow sexy drawl. Not only that, as he slowly enunciated each word, I could see that he had a pierced tongue with a round stud in it. I knew I would never be able to look at little Theo in Cosby show reruns the same way again.

My case was brought by a California company that had invented a device called the "Tiggler" a number of years before the "Tongue Joy" device came on the market. The claim in the patent infringement action that the "Tiggler" inventor filed was that sometime later, the "Tongue Joy" company began to market the infringing device which could be used whether you had a pierced tongue or not. It seems that unlike the "Tiggler" which could only be used with pierced tongues, the "Tongue Joy" could also attach to your tongue with rubber bands for those who hadn't gotten around to piercing their tongue yet or for the squeamish who just didn't have the nerve to do so. The inventor of the "Tiggler" was apparently having some success in the marketing of his patented product, when all of a sudden, this competitor allegedly stole their idea and developed the competing "Tongue Joy" device.

While I was in court listening to their preliminary explanations about the product and the nature of the dispute, a member of my staff sent me an email requesting that I bring the products back to chambers during a break so they could examine them . . . . just in case I needed some help analyzing the claims in the patent. You can rest assured that they had never asked me to bring any oil field equipment or tools back into chambers to examine in any of my other patent cases.

After the preliminary hearing the litigation really started heating up. The parties began the discovery process which involved taking testimony from various witnesses by means of a deposition. This type of discovery is generally done at the offices of one of the lawyers. On one such occasion the lawyers were in San Francisco taking the deposition of an important witness. Occasionally during a deposition a dispute will arise about the questions being asked of a witness. When that occurs, the lawyers are free to call me and ask for my assistance in resolving the dispute. Generally speaking, the dispute centers around the legitimacy of a question or an objection to a question that is being asked by one of the lawyers. When that happens, I will rule by phone so the lawyers won't have to delay their work.

In this case it seems that there was a rather heated exchange between the lawyers during the questioning of one witness. As astonishing as it might sound, the lawyers actually came to blows and starting beating each other up. Somebody called me while this melee was going on and asked me if I could help calm the situation down. They put me on speaker phone so I could talk to the lawyers. As I tried to diffuse the situation over the phone I felt more like I was talking to preschoolers than to grown men.

"Mr. so and so, please stop hitting the other counsel."

"But he hit me first, your honor."

"So and so, did you hit him first?"

"Yes, but only because he was saying something really stupid that made me mad."

And then I heard some more scuffling and people screaming. Finally somebody picked up the phone and told me that they were at it again, so I instructed them to just call the police. What I didn't know at the time was that the building they were in had previously been the scene of a shooting. It seems that there was a rather nasty divorce going on and the husband was fed up with his wife's lawyer. Apparently he thought the best course of action was just to go shoot the lawyer. Too much Shakespeare I guess. As a result, the building had a notorious reputation.

When the police were alerted to an altercation in the building between two lawyers they assumed the worse. In a matter of minutes a SWAT team had descended on the building. The police found no weapons of mass destruction, but the two lawyers had a lot of answering to do before the police were satisfied that day. In the end, we still had the problem of needing to finish the testimony of the witness, so I convinced another federal judge in San Francisco to babysit my lawyers by allowing them to work at the courthouse so they could stay out of trouble. It felt very similar to sending a child off for a time out. At the end of the day, I was thankful that I had just finished reading a new parenting book. The techniques described in the book work on small children and people who act like small children. Who knew that judging and mothering were the same thing just with bigger kids.

At the end of this case I knew I would never be able to look at somebody with a pierced tongue the same way again. But it made me think about adding one more item to the list of things to observe about potential suitors. Nice shoes? Check. Nice teeth? Check. Pierced tongue????

Chapter 13

Bad Shot

In every case where there will be a trial by jury, there is a procedure at the inception of the case where we choose the jury known as Voir Dire. During this stage of the trial proceeding it is the responsibility of the judge to select the jury by asking questions that are designed to determine if a potential juror might pre-judge the issues in a case because of their own previous experiences. For instance, if a potential juror has had serious problems in their family with someone who was addicted to drugs, it might be difficult for them to be fair and impartial in a case involving someone accused of selling drugs. Consequently, the questions that I ask can be very personal in nature. Most of the time the prospective jurors are willing to answer the questions in front of the other jury members. Occasionally, however, a juror will raise their hand and indicate that they want to speak to me and the lawyers privately. On such occasions we arrange for jurors to be brought back into the courtroom at a later time.

Sometimes the matters that jurors reveal to us during these sessions are very private, for example, details about a medical condition that might interfere with their jury service. You would be shocked to know how many hernias I have heard about. Sometimes they just want to tell me about a person in their family who was involved in the criminal justice system. The wayward son or daughter who just can't get it together. Occasionally, however, I hear something that I haven't ever heard before about a friend or family member who has died under circumstances that would impact their ability to sit on the jury, or a once in a lifetime business deal that they just don't want to miss, but don't want anybody else to know about.

On one such occasion I had a lady stand up in response to my question about whether anyone had been involved in the criminal justice system. She looked to be in her early forties and was very professionally dressed. When I called on her, she asked if she could talk to me about her situation outside of the presence of the rest of the jury. When the general questions of the panel were finished, I called her in to talk with her.

When she first started speaking her voice was very low, almost a conspiratorial whisper. She indicated that she wanted to tell me about a situation where she had been involved in the criminal justice system. It seems that her estranged husband had broken into her house one evening. And then to my great surprise, when I asked what happened, she calmly said, "I shot him." But what happened next completely threw me. She then proceeded to tell me that the entire incident had been reported on Channel 13 News.

"Wow," I said. I then mustered the nerve to ask my next question.

"Did he die?"

"No," she replied, "I wasn't a good enough shot."

"Ok. Well thank you very much, Mrs . . . .". I began to say as I glanced down at the jury list to find her name. When I finally found the name, I couldn't believe my eyes. Was this some sort of joke or is life just stranger than fiction? I stuttered as I asked, "Is this your real name?"

"Yes," she said.

"Ok, then, well thank you very much Mrs. Shotwell."

As a result of that exchange, I almost forgot to ask the most important question. Before letting her go, I regained my composure and asked. "By the way, did you get charged criminally in the incident?"

"No, I didn't. But he did. I'm just mad that all he got was probation after he broke into my house."

I was reminded of an old saying we have here in Texas. If you'd killed him when you met him, you'd be out by now.

CHAPTER 14

The "Niger" is Guilty

There is nothing that I hate worse than a bigot. Oh, actually, there is, a stupid bigot (but that's probably redundant). And there is probably nothing that a bigot hates worse than a black, female, federal judge when he has jury duty. I can (in the immortal words of Eddie Murphy in the movie 48 hours) be their worst nightmare. Still, I'm caught off guard when someone is blatantly prejudiced and brings it to me in my courtroom. It happened to me during a well-publicized case involving a black defendant. Because of the sensitive nature of the case, we decided to have the jurors fill out questionnaires in advance to determine if there was anyone we should eliminate as a prospective juror.

The initial questions were designed to help us determine if any prospective juror had heard so much about the case in the media that it might be impossible for them to render a verdict based solely on the evidence presented at trial. Had they been swayed so much by things that they may have heard outside of the courtroom that it would be difficult for them to be a fair and impartial juror? We asked each juror if they had read or heard anything about the case in the media and whether they had formed any conclusions about the guilt or innocence of the defendant as a result of whatever that was. Most people answered as we expected—that they had heard some media about the case, but that they understood that was not evidence and they would be willing to wait and make a decision on the basis of the evidence produced at trial. But of course, there is always one guy who is determined to rock the boat.

My boat rocker was a bigoted man who decided that he would use the questionnaire to not only let us know how he felt, but to hopefully get out of jury duty at the same time. In response to the question about whether he had heard or read anything that caused him to form a conclusion about the guilt or innocence of the defendant, this juror answered as follows: "The Niger is Guilty". Now you know why I said that calling somebody both a bigot and stupid is redundant. I suppose the juror probably thought that response alone would get him out of jury duty, but then he wasn't expecting to have to face me again after he wrote it. That was a significant miscalculation. I go out of my way to be nice to every prospective juror. After all, they are performing a public duty. But this guy made me want to come down off the bench and grab him by the ear like teachers used to do and make him write a hundred times on the blackboard, "I will not be a bigot". I decided it would be better if I just talked to him about his, uh . . . indiscretion.

I called the juror into the courtroom to talk to him individually about his questionnaire, as I did with every juror. I could tell when he came into the courtroom that he was a little nervous. I wondered what might be going through his head. Was he wondering if I had noticed his little slur? Did he think that he would get excused immediately because of what he wrote? Or was he hoping that I hadn't noticed what he wrote and that we were just going to have pleasant conversation? Funny thing, but something about stepping into the austerity of a courtroom makes everybody want to be nice and cooperative. Our conversation began something like this.

Me: "Good afternoon, sir."

He: "Good afternoon."

He replied in a muffled voice that sounded like something was caught in his throat.

Me: "Thank you for filling out our questionnaire; it makes the jury selection process easier for us."

He: "Uh, ok."

Was that a little bead of sweat that I just saw running down the side of his face? Don't be nervous now. You were the big dog when you were filling out your questionnaire, so don't punk out on me now.

Me: "One of the things that we need to be sure about is that you haven't already formed any conclusions about the outcome of this case. You haven't done that have you?"

He: "Oh no. No, I haven't."

Me: "Are you sure, because you wrote something that made me think that you have?"

He begins to wring his hands nervously, but doesn't answer me. But now he knows I have seen it.

Me: "In answer to question ten you wrote, 'The niger is guilty'. The Niger is a river in Egypt. Did you know that?"

He can barely lift his head to meet my eyes as he replies.

He: "No."

Me: "Did you mean to write nigger?"

He: no answer

Me: ". . . because nigger is spelled n-i-g-g-e-r and you spelled it with only one g. Did you realize that?"

He: "No."

Me: "Of course you didn't. Now by nigger, I suppose you mean the black man who is accused as a defendant in this case, correct?"

He: "Uh, I guess."

Me: "And you wanted me to know how you felt about him, huh?"

He: "Well, I dunno."

Me: "And do you have children?"

I know I should have stopped, but I just couldn't stand the fact that he thought it was ok to send in this ridiculous answer and that he thought there would be no consequences for his actions.

He: "Uh, yes, I have a son."

Me: "And I bet your son would be so proud to see what you wrote on your jury questionnaire."

He: "Probably not."

By this time the prospective juror was sweating profusely and I knew I had made my point. Not only was he continuing to wring his hands, but they were even shaking a little. So I decided to end his ordeal by offering him one piece of advice.

"Better to be silent and thought a fool than to speak and remove all doubt."

It wasn't entirely clear to me that he understood the point and that should not have surprised me. After all, even if I hadn't been the judge on this case, what good did he expect would come from making such a blatantly prejudiced and ridiculous statement? Did he imagine that he would be lucky enough to encounter another judge who was as bigoted as he that might come down off the bench and give him a high five? Or did he just think that the lawyers would be disgusted by his statement and let him go without issue? It reminded me of that crazy skit that Eddie Murphy did on Saturday Night Live where he dressed in white face to see what happened in an alternative universe where everyone thought black people weren't around and they could say anything they wanted to with no repercussions.

I wanted to say more to him, but ultimately I decided to let him go. I had made my point, and he had gotten it. It was not ok to use racial slurs in a courtroom setting and that if you do, the statement might be thrown back at you by someone who turns out to be your worst nightmare. Most of all, if you're going to be a bigot, at least learn how to spell! But I guess that would be asking too much.

CHAPTER 15

Can I Keep My Jet and Other Ridiculous Requests

When defendants are released pending trial, there are many restrictions that are placed upon them. They are prohibited from possessing weapons; they are prohibited from maintaining contact with people who are involved with crime; they have to report where they live and where they work and also anything that is requested about their financial situation. They might also have to give up or forfeit anything in their possession that was associated with the crime such as guns, cash, cars and houses. I once had a group of defendants that had managed to amass quite a few material possessions that were clearly the fruit of their ill-gotten gains. These defendants knew that the government would seek forfeiture of many of those items, and rightfully so, but it didn't stop them from asking, "Can my wife keep her diamond necklace", "Can I keep my Ferrari", and the piece de resistance, "Can I keep my jet". Of course nobody was going to invite them to any more parties, so the necklace was really unnecessary and giving somebody on bond a fast car and a plane reminded me of Little Red Riding Hood—the better to run away from you my dear. Request Denied.

One defendant I had was re-incarcerated after violating his terms of release. He was given every chance to do the right thing but he just wouldn't cooperate. He railed against his probation officer for causing him to be put back into custody. When he saw that wasn't likely to get him an earlier release, he decided to go to the bible for some help. He demanded that I release him from custody so he could make love to a woman like it says in the bible. I wasn't able to find that specific passage of scripture and he wasn't able to show me where it was either. Request Denied.

One of the pleasures of my job is the ability to marry people. Generally it is my policy to only marry people that I know and have some relationship with. Over the years I have joyfully participated in the wedding ceremonies of several of my clerks and interns. I have also had the pleasure of marrying several ladies from my breakfast club over the years. On one occasion, a fellow judge called to ask if I would marry a couple that she wanted to send over. It seemed that she was scheduled to sentence the man that day and didn't feel right performing the marriage ceremony herself. I agreed and she sent the couple over to see me. As she had informed me, they asked if I would be willing to marry them. The young woman was tall and very striking. I remember her because she shared the name of a very popular television actress. I didn't want to be nosy, but I certainly wondered what was motivating her to marry somebody about to be sentenced to prison. Fortunately that duty didn't fall to me and I did what I was asked to do by uniting the happy couple. Following the ceremony they went across the hall so the groom could be sentenced. He got twenty-four years. That had to be the shortest honeymoon on record. This was a request that I granted, but that I thought should have been denied.

As judges we know that being called for jury duty is not one of life's great pleasures, but it is one of life's great privileges as citizens. Nonetheless, I try to soften the blow and the clear imposition on a juror's time by being as polite, friendly and humorous as the circumstances permit. Even so, there will always be jurors that just don't want to be there. Most of the time this is due to work or other commitments and of course there are some circumstances that justify excusing someone from jury duty. Otherwise, they just have to serve. One juror had let me know during the jury selection process that he just wasn't happy to be there and wanted to be excused. I listened patiently to his explanation, but at the end of the day there just was no basis for excusing him. There still was a chance that the lawyers would strike him, but as it turned out, they didn't do so. As a result he ended up on the jury. After he was selected, I know what he wanted to say was please let me off this jury because I don't want to be here, but that would have been inappropriate. Instead, he decided to ask for his removal in a most unusual way. Right after I swore the jury in, he raised his thumb and pointer finger up and simulated a gun and pointed them at me and said POW"! I'm sure that what he meant to say by that gesture was, "Can I get off the jury, pretty please", but to the marshals who were there to protect me, it looked like, "If I had a gun I would shoot you". His unspoken request to be excused from the jury was quickly granted—by the marshals, but at the end of the day, I know he wished he had never made it.

Federal judges like their anonymity. Everybody knows what Judge Ito looks like, but I don't know a single federal judge who has ever allowed a camera in their courtroom. Whenever I have a high profile case, there is always a request to allow a camera in the courtroom but the answer is always no. You cannot stop artists from coming into the courtroom, however, and from time to time I have had an artist in the courtroom drawing a scene that ends up on the news. On one occasion, I had an artist in my courtroom during a well-publicized case. I really wasn't paying that much attention to her, but I should have. As it turns out, I was having a bad hair day, so I had pulled my hair up into a ball.

Later that week my hair stylist asked me why I had allowed my picture to be shown on t.v. when my hair was such a mess. What could I say? I told her that I hadn't planned to have a bad hair day when the artist showed up. Her response was to make just one request of me. "If you have any more high profile trials, will you please come get your hair done first?" Lest you think this was her effort to protect my image, she made it clear that my bad hair days were a bad reflection on her reputation. This request was granted.

CHAPTER 16

What Would Miss Manners Say

For the most part, once I sentence someone I generally am never going to see them again. In the current atmosphere, there are far more prosecutions of people who could be your neighbors like bankers and business people and other white collar folks. One of the valuable things that I have learned from watching the prosecutions of so many white collar crimes is how to follow the commandment, "Thou Shall Not Covet". Actually, I think the commandment actually says thou shall not covet thy neighbor's wife, but generally I think that what was meant is that you are not supposed to covet anything that belongs to your neighbor—not their wife, not their home, not their expensive cars (even though there weren't any expensive cars around when God gave Moses this particular commandment).

What I hadn't considered in watching the rise in these prosecutions is that these days, living in a nice part of town is no different it seems from living in a "bad area" of town. Some of your neighbors are going to go to jail. When it happens where I live, however, it is usually referred to as a "scandal" not a "crime", and the victims are almost routinely referred to as shareholders or investors. In some parts of town people talk about the possibility of spending time in a maximum security prison, but in the white collar crime world, the hope is always for what is sometimes referred to as "club fed". Call it what you may, prison is prison. Twenty-four-seven, somebody else is telling you what to do and when to do it. You are told when to get up, when to eat, when to shower, when you can use the restroom, the phone or the library and when to go to bed. Both your work schedule and your recreation time are tightly controlled. If you are good while you are in prison, as most white collar criminal defendants are, you can also earn good time credit which is applied to reduce your time and may get you an early release to a halfway house. This is where my story starts.

A prominent Houstonian had gotten himself in some trouble by over promising and under delivering on an investment opportunity he was working on. In common terms, he had committed fraud. While I did not know this man personally, I knew he came from a respectable Houston family and that they were devastated by the thought of him going to prison. At the end of the day, however, he ended up serving far less time than he might have by cooperating with the government—essentially telling on some other people—in exchange for a plea agreement that enabled him to obtain a lighter sentence. (it's a lot easier telling on people when they are white collar criminals than it is to tell on other drug dealers). Even though he had charges pending against him in more than one court, it fell to me ultimately to actually sentence him. Consistent with his plea agreement with the government, I gave him the reduced sentence that he had negotiated and sent him off to prison.

Generally speaking, after I sentence someone to prison, I don't really hear anything else about them until they are released to a term of supervision. That is a probationary type period that follows their incarceration in which we monitor them closely as they reintegrate into the free world. I never thought I would hear anything about this particular defendant while he was on supervision. As expected, he was first released to a halfway house and then eventually to supervision without incident.

Then one day I was playing in a charity golf tournament. As I was waiting for the tournament to begin, I was talking to one of my friends. While we were talking, I noticed his eyes get big as he looked over my shoulder. Then he said, "Don't look now, but I think a guy you sentenced to prison is playing in this tournament and he is walking this way." After he identified who he was talking about, I froze in place. The last thing that I wanted to have to do while I was playing golf was to confront somebody that I had sentenced to prison. For many years, there had not been much chance of that ever happening. The possibility of my running into a drug dealer or bank robber in a social situation was slim to none. But now that we were sending so many white collar criminals to prison, the possibility of running into someone I had sentenced had increased greatly. Unfortunately, I had never had a chance to consider how I would or should react to this possibility in a social setting.

I tried as hard as I could to make myself invisible, but I had left my invisibility cloak at home that day. I didn't turn around and I wasn't moving anything except my lips.

"Do you think he sees me?" I asked my friend,

"I don't know but he's still coming this way," he replied.

"How close is he now?"

"He's closing in on you. I think he sees you. He's almost right behind you!"

Finally I felt the dreaded tap on the shoulder. I was hoping he hadn't seen me, but I was not going to be that fortunate. I could hardly believe it, but I should have known this day would come. For some defendants, time away in prison is like going off for some medical treatment. Once they are finished, they resume the life that they had before with few if any changes in their lives. This man had obviously been a golfer and here he was, after his release, playing golf in a charity tournament.

I knew I had to turn around, but I did so slowly, trying to formulate what I would say.

"Hello there," I said as nonchalantly as possible.

"Hi, Judge Gilmore."

Darn, he recognized me. I was still hoping that maybe he didn't recognize me and I wouldn't have to engage him in conversation. No such luck. He stuck his hand out to shake mine and after making sure that he didn't have a booby trap, I took his hand and shook it. Now I wondered what would happen next.

"Are you playing in the tournament?" I asked, trying to make small talk.

"Yes, I am," he replied. "But that's not what I wanted to talk to you about."

Ok, here it goes, I thought. He is going to curse me or slap me or curse me and then slap me. Whatever way it went, it didn't seem like it could possibly be good.

"I just wanted to say thank you."

"Excuse me?" I asked.

"I just wanted to say thank you. I know that you didn't have to go along with that plea agreement that I worked out with the government and that I could have gotten a lot more time. I just want to say thank you for giving me the sentence that you did so that I could pay my debt to society and get back to my family."

I was completely stumped. What could possibly be the response to someone who is thanking you when the only thing that you have ever done for them is send them to prison.? What would Miss Manners say about this? I wondered if I should stick with you're welcome. In Spanish, which we use a lot here in Texas, the response is "de nada"—it was nothing. No, that didn't sound right. A more formal response might be "not at all", a less formal response might be "no problem". As the rules of etiquette swirled through my head, somehow none of those tried and true responses seemed to fit the occasion. This man was sincerely thanking me for sending him to prison and I was at a loss for words—something that almost never happens to me. I felt like I had to say something. If I said nothing, he might think me rude or arrogant. If I said the wrong thing he might think me rude or arrogant. What's a judge to do?!

Finally, I looked him in his eyes, which wasn't hard considering he was still gripping my hand and I said, "And how is your lovely wife?" Now I didn't really know his wife so I didn't know if she was lovely or not. It just seemed like the only thing to say at the time. He smiled and shook my hand and we both went on to play our rounds of golf.

I would certainly have failed the Miss Manners etiquette course that day. After this incident, I looked to see what Miss Manners would have said. Her advice was not to mess with convention and just say, "you're welcome". After the fact I thought of another response that I wish I had used, "don't mention it". It seemed to me that would have been the most appropriate response, because in reality, some thank you's are better left unsaid.

CHAPTER 17

It's Great to be a mentor (I think)

As you might imagine, I am asked to speak to a lot of student groups. I generally like this part of my job. I feel that it is important to be seen in the community and not hide in our "ivory towers". So I get out and I speak at schools, churches and for non profit organizations that help kids. Occasionally, students will actually come to the courthouse to watch court proceedings and to see me in court. That provides a great opportunity for me to talk to them after they have actually had a chance to see what court is really like.

One summer I was in the middle of trying one of the Enron criminal cases when a group of students from a program called "Communities in Schools" came to watch part of the trial. Afterward, I joined them for lunch at a local law firm. I talked about the courts, about justice and about how I became a federal judge. Finally, I asked if they had any questions and they peppered me with a number of thoughtful inquiries. Just as I thought I was finished, one young lady raised her hand and said she had a question to ask. I said ok and she asked, "Do you play golf?" Now that was admittedly the most intriguing question that I have ever gotten from a student in that type of setting. I said that I did and she raised her hand again and asked if I wanted to play golf with her. I was a little hesitant, but said o.k, sure, figuring that I would probably never hear from her again. Then she told me that she was number two in her division. I thought, this is ridiculous. Some little Michelle Wie wanna-be just wants to kick my butt in golf. So I smiled one of those fake smiles and gave her my card, hoping against hope that I would never hear from her again. But, I would have no such luck.

Almost immediately, this girl started calling my office asking my secretary if she could set up a time to play golf with me. The first couple of times I told my secretary to say I wasn't there. Then I suggested that she tell her that I didn't work there anymore. Neither ploy was working because she just kept calling. Finally, my secretary decided to take matters into her own hands and set up a golf game for us and told me about it after the fact. On the day we were scheduled to play, I got so nervous. I knew that this young lady, who was second in her division, was going to wipe up the course with me. We went to the driving range and she was at the practice mat behind me so I wasn't facing her while we practiced. A couple of times I noticed balls coming across in front of me, but I assumed that they were from another golfer further down from us without ever looking up. Finally, it was time for us to go play. I was a little nervous, but I decided to tee off first. It was a difficult hole that required you to hit over a large ravine, but I connected on my first shot and my ball landed in the middle of the fairway near the 150-yard marker. I breathed a sigh of relief that I hadn't embarrassed myself as soon as we started. Then it was my little friend's turn to hit. On her very first shot she hit the top of the ball and instead of taking off, it trickled down the hill before disappearing into the ravine. No big deal I thought. Lots of people misfire on the first shot of the day. I encouraged her to take a mulligan, which is a do-over, and try it again. But on her second try, the ball trickled down the hill and into the ravine again. One mulligan is fair, but two is really cheating so I suggested that we just move on so as not to hold up the players behind us. We got to my ball and I hit it right onto the green where it belonged. She dropped her ball close to where mine had been and proceeded to hit it off the fairway into the rough grass on the side. Of course that meant her ball was nowhere to be found. I told her she could just putt from where my ball landed. Even her putting was horrible. I was beginning to wonder by now whether she had just flat out lied about being able to play golf. Nobody who was second in their division could be having this bad of a day. As we got back into the cart I asked her to be sure, "Sweetie, I thought you said that you were second in your division?" She replied, "Yes, I was. My school played this other school and we came in second." Oh, now I got it. She came in second in a tournament that only had two schools, so in essence she came in last! She didn't lie. She said she was second! She just didn't say she was the second in a two team tournament! Her game never got better, so finally in frustration we had to quit after about six holes before we got kicked off the course for delaying the pace of play.

I hoped after that experience she would never have the nerve to call me again, but I was wrong. After that she decided that I had been so patient with her during our golf outing that she was going to give me the chance to be her permanent mentor. The thought that came to mind for me was, no good deed goes unpunished. Yet I had to admit that there was something I liked about this girl having enough nerve to ask a federal judge to play golf when she really couldn't play at all. That took moxie. And so our mentor—mentee relationship began. I helped her with college admission applications and scholarship information and cheered her on when she was accepted to a local community college. She called periodically for advice and counsel and I encouraged her in her studies.

One day when she called she didn't sound like her normal upbeat self. She finally confessed that her boyfriend—with the emphasis on boy—had been beating her. I was shocked and dismayed by what she told me and I gave her this very blunt advice. "If he beat your ass once, he's going to beat your ass again. Leave him alone." I guess she didn't like what I had to say because after that I didn't hear from her for about a year. I tried reaching out to her but her phones were disconnected and her internet address didn't even work. When she finally called, she left word that it was an emergency and she needed to speak to me right away. She asked for my help to get her baby back from children's protective services which is the agency that helps abused children. What baby?! And why is the baby in CPS custody? It turns out that not only had she stayed with her abuser, but she had a baby by him too. She had dropped the baby off to visit him and he got mad because the baby was crying too much so he broke his arm. Now the baby had been taken away from her. This was all just too much to process in a two minute conversation, but this was the awful reality she had created for herself. I didn't know when I signed on for this mentoring job that part of my role would be to help retrieve a baby from children's protective services, but I agreed to try to help her.

A local district attorney called and asked me to testify at a hearing that would ensure the boyfriend would be taken into custody and baby would be released to my mentee. When I showed up, she interviewed me about my potential testimony. Of course I had never witnessed the abuse to my mentee and only knew of it second-hand from our conversation. This of course would be hearsay under the rules of evidence and would not be permissible testimony. I assured that district attorney that as a federal judge I understood very well the rules of evidence and that she should put me on the stand anyway because of course I could still testify about what I said even if I was not permitted to say what she told me. I sat in court for several hours waiting for her case to be called listening to the drama of other people's lives. I had been in the federal courts for so long that I didn't have a clue about the every day drama that played out in courts like this. Jerry Springer had nothing on these folks. Finally it was time for our case.

When it was my time to testify, I could see that the judge was surprised when I was called to the stand. I hoped that would be good. I began by describing my role as her mentor over the years; how we had met at the school program; how I had tried to help and encourage her in her studies. Then it was time for me to try to discuss the abusive boyfriend. The exchange went like this.

D.A. : Did she ever call you and talk to you about her boyfriend?

Me: Yes

D.A.: And what did she tell you?

Me: That he was beating her up.

Opposing Counsel: Objection, hearsay!

Court: Sustained.

Now of course I knew that testimony was hearsay. But I also knew how to get that evidence in.

D.A.: Without telling us anything she told you, please tell the court what advice, if any, you gave her.

Me: I said, if he beat your ass once, he's going to beat your ass again.

I thought the judge was going to pass out. But in the end, we accomplished our objective. She got her baby back. She later called to thank me and told me that after seeing what a good life my son had after I adopted him that she had decided to give her baby up for adoption so that he could have a good life too. It made me cry. It's good to be a mentor.

Chapter 18

I'm a Federal Judge

The good thing about this job is having the United States marshals to look out for you. The bad thing about this job is having the United States marshals to look out for you. Because it is the job of the marshals to make sure that the judges are safe, as a rule, they really don't want you going places where you might be endangered in any way. Most of the time that doesn't put too many restrictions on the places you can go, but even in some of the nicest places you meet some crazy people.

One evening I went to a downtown restaurant to take a girlfriend of mine out for a drink for her birthday. We sat at the bar chatting for a while and then I excused myself to go to the restroom. When I returned, there was some guy standing there chatting her up. When I sat down, he turned to me and said, "What are you girls up to tonight?" He was so impressed with himself that he didn't even notice that both of us were rolling our eyes. We explained to him that we were having a drink for my friend's birthday and implied that we would rather be alone. But some people don't understand subtlety so he just kept right on talking as if we hadn't said anything.

"A bunch of us are going upstairs to another bar. You should join us."

"Why would we want to do that?" we asked.

"Because it's the kind of place where you can reinvent yourself."

"Reinvent yourself? What does that mean?" I inquired.

"Well, just last week I was up there and I told the people that I met that I was a federal judge."

"You don't say," I asked in surprise.

"Yeah, really."

"And they believed you, huh?" I asked again.

"Yeah, of course."

Now at this point you should know that there is nothing about this man's appearance that would make you think he could be a federal judge. He had on a short sleeved dress shirt, which is itself an oxymoron. He had a kind of country and western too much hair on top hairdo and he had on some pants that looked like they were made of knit polyester. He wasn't even wearing a sports jacket!

"Well, that is interesting," I continued. "I think that I will go upstairs and say I'm a federal judge."

"No, no, no," he said, shaking his head. "It has to be something believable. It can't be that far fetched."

My friend and I almost choked on our drinks at this point, but instead we decided to just keep playing along.

"Well, I think I'm going to say I'm a trial lawyer," my girlfriend, who actually was a trial lawyer, said in response.

"No, no, you girls don't understand. If you want to say you work in a legal field, just say that you are probation officers or something, ok?"

"But I really liked that federal judge title," I insisted.

"No, like I said, you have to choose something believable. I'm going on upstairs. I hope that you girls decide to come upstairs."

We could barely keep a straight face as we watched him saunter upstairs. As soon as he was out of earshot, we broke out laughing.

"Oh my God, can you believe that guy said he was a federal judge?" I asked my friend.

"Do you have your badge with you today?" she asked.

Until that day, the badge had been of limited usefulness. Oh, sure, I kept my driver's license inside the wallet part just in case I got stopped by the police so that I could accidentally flash it while I was retrieving my license. And it had stopped one person, who I am sure was a fake cop, from bothering me. But beyond those two ticket saving and possibly life-saving events, I hadn't really had much opportunity to use my badge. All of that changed that night.

And so I smiled a mischievous smile and said to my friend, "Of course I have my badge."

"Then let's go ruin that guy's night," she replied.

We went upstairs, trying to look as innocent as possible. When Mr. Reinvent Yourself spotted us, he came rushing over to greet us.

"I'm so glad you girls decided to come upstairs," he beamed. "How should I introduce you?"

I repeated my earlier statement that I would like to be introduced as a federal judge. Again, my would-be host implored me to pick something more realistic. Alas, yet another example of the soft bigotry of low expectations. I knew that there was only one thing I could do; hit him hard.

"I brought something that I thought might help people believe I was a federal judge," I said almost sheepishly. And then I pulled out my badge and held it for him to see. Bam!

His eyes got as big as saucers as he read out loud, "United States District Judge. Oh, my God, you really are a federal judge?!"

"Yes," I replied.

And then he turned to my friend and said, "and I guess you are a trial lawyer."

"Yes," she said.

At that moment I was reminded of the episode of Sex and the City where Miranda decided to start telling people she was a flight attendant because she thought being a female lawyer just didn't sound sexy enough. As tempting as it was, I decided I was way too much of a diva to buy into this guy's underestimation of me based on the way I looked. I daresay that after our encounter our would-be-host was going to have to pick another profession to impersonate from then on. And even though I had long since come to understand that being a judge only defined what I did, not who I am, that night as I walked away, I was glad that I was a federal judge.

CHAPTER 19

No, Really I'm a Federal Judge

Now, I'm a federal judge and quite possibly may be a diva, but I don't think that I always act like a diva. Some of the judges I work with, who are never called divas, don't even open their own e-mails, and several of my colleagues don't even go out to get their own lunch. I have on a rare occasion asked my judicial assistant or clerks to grab something for me to eat when they were already going to get something for themselves. Most of the time, however, if I want something to eat, I'll go get it myself and use that as an opportunity to stretch my legs and get some sun and fresh air.

The federal courthouse in Houston is located in a building that was built sometime in 1960—before the end of the cold war—and is the only bomb shelter in downtown Houston. It is big, it is square, it is ugly and it has absolutely no personality. The judges and their staff and the delivery people and our prisoners all enter the building from the same area behind the courthouse where there is a gated parking lot and a delivery dock, which means that the court security officers are particularly diligent about monitoring who enters through the back gates. There are two large electronic gates to drive through and three pedestrian gates that you can open with an access card.

One day I decided to go out and get myself some soup for lunch. I walked across the street being careful to cross at the corner to avoid the cars that often whipped around the corner threatening to mow down some unsuspecting pedestrian. It was a pleasant day outside and I was glad for the few minutes of sunshine on my face. After I got my soup, I managed to make my way back across the street without getting hit again. I had my soup in one hand and my badge with the card key for access to the pedestrian gate in the other.

As I approached the pedestrian gate, I noticed a young man in front of me who was about to enter the gate. He looked like a generic law clerk, a young, red faced, blond man of about twenty five years of age with a suit on. Now I say generic law clerk, but I must insert here that he looks like a generic law clerk for a trial judge, all of whom insist that their law clerks wear appropriate business attire to work so that they are properly attired for court. In my chambers, the female law clerks area also required to always have on lipstick when they are in court. We have to represent after all. The law clerks of the appellate judges who practically never see the inside of a courtroom dress like they are either going to a rock concert or like they just got out of bed in ragged jeans and tee-shirts and flip flops that really have no place in a federal courthouse . . . . but I digress. Anyway, getting back to Mr. clean cut—he looked like he was fresh out of law school and the ink was not quite dry on his diploma. The kind of kid who thinks he knows everything, but really knows just enough to be dangerous.

He reached the gate just before I did, and used his card key to open it. Great, I thought to myself. Now I won't have to juggle holding my soup upright to use my card key to open the gate. As he swung the gate open, I reached up to grab it and proceed into the parking lot behind him. But as I did, he turned abruptly to face me and blocked my way. At first I thought that he accidentally blocked my way and so I moved to one side to continue entering. To my great surprise, he moved with me as if we were doing some bizarre dance and blocked my way again. This time it finally dawned on me that he was trying to keep me out of the gated parking area.

"Excuse me," I said sternly.

To which the young man replied, "You have to have permission to enter through this gate. Do you belong here?"

What?! I didn't look like I belonged there? Was I too tall? Now, I know I don't look like the other federal judges in my building. I have a lot more hair than many of them, and I am a lot cuter than all of the boy judges. But certainly I should stand out as somebody noticeable to the new clerks who begin working there. I am, after all, the only African American woman federal district judge in the entire fifth circuit which comprises, Texas, Louisiana and Mississippi! Just like the guy in the bar, here was another man who had decided to underestimate me based on the way I looked. Moreover, this young man had suddenly decided that the court security officers manning the back dock and back gate area, who always had the area under surveillance, and were in fact watching me right then, weren't doing a good enough job of keeping out the riff-raff. If he felt that he needed to supplement their security efforts by standing in the way of any potential intruders who didn't look like they belonged, then I think he should have, at a minimum, familiarized himself with the identity of the judges who worked there, just like the real court security officers do when they start their jobs. But no, this young man had looked me over, sized me up, decided that I was the wrong sex or the wrong race or the wrong height and just as the guy in the bar had done, decided that it was just too far fetched to think that I might actually be a federal judge or even some other court employee. I was somewhere between shock and rage as I stared him down in this face off.

"Who are you?", I demanded.

"I'm Mike K . . . . ," he said somewhat indignantly.

"Who are you Mike K . . . .?" I asked again.

"I'm Judge Werlein's law clerk."

At which point, I risked spilling my soup and grabbed my badge and held it up to his face and said, "I'm Judge Gilmore, please get out of my way!"

He jumped back and held the gate open for me to let me pass. At this point the mortified court security officers came running over to see if I was o.k. and to give young Mr. K . . . . the evil eye. I proceeded to my chambers to have my soup, but couldn't resist sending Mike K . . . . an email that simply said, "I really am a federal judge. If you want to make sure that the people coming in the back gate aren't coming in here to bother me or my colleagues, come around and meet all of us so you will know what we look like and you won't make the mistake you made today again."

What's a diva to do? I told Judge Werlein that since he looked like the judge from central casting with white hair and glasses, that I was going to substitute his picture for mine on the court web site. Of course, he might look more like a judge, but since I'm cuter and have better hair, I think I'll stick with my own picture and hope for more enlightened gate monitors.

CHAPTER 20

You are not the Judge

When I was still practicing law and working as a trial attorney, my time and my life were controlled for the most part by some judge. They dictated when you could come and go by the enforcement of the trial schedule. Working as a trial lawyer often meant sixteen hour days. After you spent a full day in court, you still had to come back to the office at night to prepare for the next day. One of the things that I have really appreciated about being a judge is that it gives me the time and flexibility that I need as a mother.

My son apparently came to appreciate at a very young age that as a judge I could almost always be there for him since I was the one setting the schedule. He got used to the fact that I could sign up for field trips and class parties and cafeteria duty. To him, my role as a judge was entirely secondary to his needs as my son.

One evening when he was about three years old we were doing some grocery shopping. As I pushed him along in a basket, trying to avoid the aisles with the sugary snacks, he chatted on about all the things he had done in school that day. As we proceeded down one aisle, we passed a lawyer that recognized me who greeted me as we passed, "Hello judge." As we continued our shopping, we passed someone else who apparently recognized me as well who looked up as we passed and said, "Good evening, judge." It must have been a busy shopping night for lawyers because before too long we passed yet another one who also greeted me with a "Hello judge."

To my surprise, my son looked at me and in a completely exasperated tone said, "Mommy, why are all those people calling you judge? You are not the judge at night time! Can't they see it is dark outside? At night time you are not the judge, you are just my mamma!"

"But honey, I'm not their mamma," I replied. Then I imagined some lawyer walking toward me in the grocery store shouting out, "Hey mamma." Not likely I guess.

He was apparently unconvinced and spent the rest of the evening glaring at everyone who passed us and daring anyone else to call me judge.

When my son was a little older, the mother of one of his friends stopped me at school. She asked me what I wanted the kids to call me. As much as I stand on formality in a courtroom setting, I am equally casual outside of court. I sheepishly responded that for the most part they called me Vanessa and that I was ok with that. Then she said something that completely changed my attitude. She related to me that she had a girlfriend who was a doctor who was close enough to her children to be referred to as Aunt Mary. She wanted them to understand, however, that women could be doctors so she had her children refer to her as Dr. Mary. She suggested that Judge Vanessa would serve the same purpose.

Following her suggestion, the next weekend my son's best friend came over for a play date. He and my son had played together almost every week since they started going to mothers' day out together as infants. When he came in and said, "Hi Vanessa" as he usually did, I informed him that from then on, I would prefer it if he referred to me as Judge Vanessa. To my complete and utter surprise he responded by asking, "You're a judge?" From that point on I have been "Judge Vanessa" or "Judge V" to all of the kids.

When I speak at elementary schools, however, I ask not to be introduced as a judge. That allows me to do a little exercise with the children before I speak. I ask the students to close their eyes and imagine that they are in a courtroom. I loudly rap on the desk with my gavel and announce the entry of the judge into the courtroom. I describe a scene where the judge is coming in wearing flowing black robes, climbing the steps, taking a seat in a large chair behind a bench and instructing everyone that they may be seated. Then I ask the children to keep their eyes closed and describe the judge to me. They start yelling out their answers—he's old, he has white hair, he is wearing glasses, he looks very mean, he's white. During that time, I slip on my own robe and then instruct them to open their eyes. For the most part the students are always shocked to see me standing there in my robe. My next question is always, "Did anybody picture somebody like me walking into the courtroom as the judge?" Surprisingly, the response is almost always the same, "You're a judge?"

Then one day a glimmer of hope. I was dropping my son off at school and his teacher stopped me to tell me that they were studying the American presidents. One of the girls apparently raised her hand to ask why there weren't any girl presidents. Before the teacher could answer, she said another girl in the class responded by saying that since I was a judge, that maybe I could be president someday. It nearly brought tears to my eyes . . . but mostly because I would rather walk through hot coals barefooted right after getting a pedicure than be president. When I asked my son about this incident that evening, he confirmed the story as his teacher had related it to me. Then he asked, "Mommy, can boys be judges too?"

Finally, some respect.

CPSIA information can be obtained
at www.ICGtesting.com
Printed in the USA
LVHW041032151218
600592LV00001B/335/P

9 781453 569511